HERE'S TO YOU

Congratulations!

You are going to be the best version of yourself!

D0868882

This book belongs to:

_____

How to Use this Book:

This book is an excellent tool to help you keep
track of your food, your weight, your exercise
and all of your amazing progress!
Each page in this resource is designed to
include your information for one day. There is
a space for you to mark the day of the week,
the date and your current weight.
Most popular diets today advocate for eating
smaller portions, six times a day. There is
space to record each fueling as well as your
lean proteins, vegetables and condiments.
Don't forget to drink your water! There is an
area for you to check off each glass.
Additionally, you can record your mood and
energy. Lastly, there is an area for you to note
your exercise.
Are you ready?

Let's go!!

STARTING POINT:

STATS

CURRENT:
Weight:
BMI :
Body Fat:
Muscle :
Size :

MEASUREMENTS

BEFORE
Chest :
Waist:
Hips :
Arms :
Thighs :
Calves :

MOTIVATION

GOAL WEIGHT

YOU'VE GOT THIS!

M T W (T) F S S

Sample Page

1 Today's Date	2 Today's Weight	3 Weight Change from Yesterday
January 1st	152.6	-.8

TODAY'S FUELINGS

1. Caramel Macchiato Shake
2. Peanut Butter Protein Bar
3. Smashed Potatoes
4. Smores Protein Bar
5. Chicken & Veggies
6. Sugar Free Pudding

Opt. Snack: Popcorn

LEAN AND GREEN MEAL

LEANS	GREENS	CONDIMENTS
7 oz Chicken Breast	1.5 Cups Broccoli	1 wedge lite Cheese

MOOD / ENERGY

Feeling great!

SLEEP ___6.5___ HRS.   WATER X XX ● ● ● ● ● ● ●

EXERCISE: NOTES

CARDIO	STRENGTH	FLEXIBILITY	OTHER
2 mile jog on the treadmill	30 reps. 5 lb hand weights	10 Min. Yoga	I mopped the floors

YOU'VE GOT THIS!

M   T   W   T   F   S   S

1 Today's Date	**2** Today's Weight	**3** Weight Change from Yesterday

TODAY'S FUELINGS

1 _____

2 _____

3 _____

4 _____

5 _____

6 _____

Opt. Snack: _____

LEAN AND GREEN MEAL

LEANS	GREENS	CONDIMENTS

MOOD / ENERGY

SLEEP _____ HRS.   WATER ○○○○○ ○○○○○

EXERCISE:

NOTES

CARDIO	STRENGTH	FLEXIBILITY	OTHER

STAY STRONG!

M T W T F S S

1 Today's Date	**2** Today's Weight	**3** Weight Change from Yesterday

TODAY'S FUELINGS

1 _____

2 _____

3 _____

4 _____

5 _____

6 _____

Opt. Snack: _____

LEAN AND GREEN MEAL

LEANS	GREENS	CONDIMENTS

MOOD / ENERGY

SLEEP _____ HRS.   WATER ○○○○○ ○○○○○

EXERCISE:

NOTES

CARDIO	STRENGTH	FLEXIBILITY	OTHER

YOU CAN DO IT!

M   T   W   T   F   S   S

1 Today's Date	**2** Today's Weight	**3** Weight Change from Yesterday

TODAY'S FUELINGS

1 _____

2 _____

3 _____

4 _____

5 _____

6 _____

Opt. Snack: _____

LEAN AND GREEN MEAL

LEANS	GREENS	CONDIMENTS

MOOD / ENERGY

SLEEP _____ HRS.   WATER ⚪⚪⚪⚪⚪ ⚪⚪⚪⚪

EXERCISE:

NOTES

CARDIO	STRENGTH	FLEXIBILITY	OTHER

LOOKIN' GOOD!

M T W T F S S

1 Today's Date	**2** Today's Weight	**3** Weight Change from Yesterday

TODAY'S FUELINGS

1 _____

2 _____

3 _____

4 _____

5 _____

6 _____

Opt. Snack: _____

LEAN AND GREEN MEAL

LEANS	GREENS	CONDIMENTS

MOOD / ENERGY

SLEEP _____ HRS.   WATER ○○○○○ ○○○○○

EXERCISE: NOTES

CARDIO	STRENGTH	FLEXIBILITY	OTHER

WOW!

M T W T F S S

1 Today's Date	**2** Today's Weight	**3** Weight Change from Yesterday

TODAY'S FUELINGS

1 _____

2 _____

3 _____

4 _____

5 _____

6 _____

Opt. Snack: _____

LEAN AND GREEN MEAL

LEANS	GREENS	CONDIMENTS

MOOD / ENERGY

SLEEP _____ HRS.   WATER ○ ○ ○ ○ ○ ○ ○ ○ ○ ○

EXERCISE:

NOTES

CARDIO	STRENGTH	FLEXIBILITY	OTHER

YOU ARE AWESOME!

M   T   W   T   F   S   S

1 Today's Date	**2** Today's Weight	**3** Weight Change from Yesterday

TODAY'S FUELINGS

1 _____

2 _____

3 _____

4 _____

5 _____

6 _____

Opt. Snack: _____

LEAN AND GREEN MEAL

LEANS	GREENS	CONDIMENTS

MOOD / ENERGY

SLEEP _____ HRS.   WATER ⚪⚪⚪⚪⚪ ⚪⚪⚪⚪⚪

EXERCISE: NOTES

CARDIO	STRENGTH	FLEXIBILITY	OTHER

WEEK 1 DONE!

M T W T F S S

1	Today's Date	2	Today's Weight	3	Weight Change from Yesterday

TODAY'S FUELINGS

1 _____

2 _____

3 _____

4 _____

5 _____

6 _____

Opt. Snack: _____

LEAN AND GREEN MEAL

LEANS	GREENS	CONDIMENTS

MOOD / ENERGY

SLEEP _____ HRS.   WATER ⬤⬤⬤⬤⬤ ⬤⬤⬤⬤

EXERCISE:

CARDIO	STRENGTH	FLEXIBILITY	OTHER

NOTES

KEEP IT GOING!

M   T   W   T   F   S   S

1 Today's Date	2 Today's Weight	3 Weight Change from Yesterday

TODAY'S FUELINGS

1 _____

2 _____

3 _____

4 _____

5 _____

6 _____

Opt. Snack: _____

LEAN AND GREEN MEAL

LEANS	GREENS	CONDIMENTS

MOOD / ENERGY

SLEEP _____ HRS.   WATER ⚪⚪⚪⚪⚪ ⚪⚪⚪⚪⚪

EXERCISE: NOTES

CARDIO	STRENGTH	FLEXIBILITY	OTHER

YOU ARE AMAZING!

M   T   W   T   F   S   S

1 Today's Date	**2** Today's Weight	**3** Weight Change from Yesterday

TODAY'S FUELINGS

1 _____

2 _____

3 _____

4 _____

5 _____

6 _____

Opt. Snack: _____

LEAN AND GREEN MEAL

LEANS	GREENS	CONDIMENTS

MOOD / ENERGY

SLEEP _____ HRS.   WATER ●●●●● ●●●●●

EXERCISE: NOTES

CARDIO	STRENGTH	FLEXIBILITY	OTHER

GREAT JOB!

M T W T F S S

1 Today's Date	**2** Today's Weight	**3** Weight Change from Yesterday

TODAY'S FUELINGS

1 _____

2 _____

3 _____

4 _____

5 _____

6 _____

Opt. Snack: _____

LEAN AND GREEN MEAL

LEANS	GREENS	CONDIMENTS

MOOD / ENERGY

SLEEP _____ HRS.   WATER ○○○○○ ○○○○○

EXERCISE:

CARDIO	STRENGTH	FLEXIBILITY	OTHER

NOTES

KEEP IT UP!

M T W T F S S

1 Today's Date	**2** Today's Weight	**3** Weight Change from Yesterday

TODAY'S FUELINGS

1 _____

2 _____

3 _____

4 _____

5 _____

6 _____

Opt. Snack: _____

LEAN AND GREEN MEAL

LEANS	GREENS	CONDIMENTS

MOOD / ENERGY

SLEEP _____ HRS.   WATER ○○○○○ ○○○○○

EXERCISE: NOTES

CARDIO	STRENGTH	FLEXIBILITY	OTHER

WAY TO GO!

M T W T F S S

1 Today's Date	**2** Today's Weight	**3** Weight Change from Yesterday

TODAY'S FUELINGS

1 _____

2 _____

3 _____

4 _____

5 _____

6 _____

Opt. Snack: _____

LEAN AND GREEN MEAL

LEANS	GREENS	CONDIMENTS

MOOD / ENERGY

SLEEP _____ HRS.   WATER ⚪⚪⚪⚪⚪ ⚪⚪⚪⚪⚪

EXERCISE: NOTES

CARDIO	STRENGTH	FLEXIBILITY	OTHER

FLEX THOSE MUSCLES!

M T W T F S S

1 Today's Date	2 Today's Weight	3 Weight Change from Yesterday

TODAY'S FUELINGS

1 _____

2 _____

3 _____

4 _____

5 _____

6 _____

Opt. Snack: _____

LEAN AND GREEN MEAL

LEANS	GREENS	CONDIMENTS

MOOD / ENERGY

SLEEP _____ HRS.   WATER ● ● ● ● ● ● ● ● ● ●

EXERCISE:

NOTES

CARDIO	STRENGTH	FLEXIBILITY	OTHER

WEEK 2 DONE!

M T W T F S S

1 Today's Date	2 Today's Weight	3 Weight Change from Yesterday

TODAY'S FUELINGS

1 _____

2 _____

3 _____

4 _____

5 _____

6 _____

Opt. Snack: _____

LEAN AND GREEN MEAL

LEANS	GREENS	CONDIMENTS

MOOD / ENERGY

SLEEP _____ HRS.   WATER ○○○○○ ○○○○○

EXERCISE:

NOTES

CARDIO	STRENGTH	FLEXIBILITY	OTHER

GO GET IT!

M T W T F S S

1 Today's Date	**2** Today's Weight	**3** Weight Change from Yesterday

TODAY'S FUELINGS

1 _____

2 _____

3 _____

4 _____

5 _____

6 _____

Opt. Snack: _____

LEAN AND GREEN MEAL

LEANS	GREENS	CONDIMENTS

MOOD / ENERGY

SLEEP _____ HRS.   WATER ● ● ● ● ●
● ● ● ● ●

EXERCISE: NOTES

CARDIO	STRENGTH	FLEXIBILITY	OTHER

GET IT DONE!

M T W T F S S

1 Today's Date	**2** Today's Weight	**3** Weight Change from Yesterday

TODAY'S FUELINGS

1 _____

2 _____

3 _____

4 _____

5 _____

6 _____

Opt. Snack: _____

LEAN AND GREEN MEAL

LEANS	GREENS	CONDIMENTS

MOOD / ENERGY

SLEEP _____ HRS.   WATER ⬤ ⬤ ⬤ ⬤ ⬤
⬤ ⬤ ⬤ ⬤ ⬤

EXERCISE: NOTES

CARDIO	STRENGTH	FLEXIBILITY	OTHER

WORK IT!

M T W T F S S

1 Today's Date	**2** Today's Weight	**3** Weight Change from Yesterday

TODAY'S FUELINGS

1 _____

2 _____

3 _____

4 _____

5 _____

6 _____

Opt. Snack: _____

LEAN AND GREEN MEAL

LEANS	GREENS	CONDIMENTS

MOOD / ENERGY

SLEEP _____ HRS.   WATER ⚪⚪⚪⚪⚪ ⚪⚪⚪⚪⚪

EXERCISE: NOTES

CARDIO	STRENGTH	FLEXIBILITY	OTHER

NICELY DONE!

M T W T F S S

1 Today's Date	**2** Today's Weight	**3** Weight Change from Yesterday

TODAY'S FUELINGS

1 _____

2 _____

3 _____

4 _____

5 _____

6 _____

Opt. Snack: _____

LEAN AND GREEN MEAL

LEANS	GREENS	CONDIMENTS

MOOD / ENERGY

SLEEP _____ HRS.   WATER ⚪⚪⚪⚪⚪ ⚪⚪⚪⚪⚪

EXERCISE: NOTES

CARDIO	STRENGTH	FLEXIBILITY	OTHER

KEEP IT MOVIN'!

M   T   W   T   F   S   S

1 Today's Date	**2** Today's Weight	**3** Weight Change from Yesterday

TODAY'S FUELINGS

1 _____

2 _____

3 _____

4 _____

5 _____

6 _____

Opt. Snack: _____

LEAN AND GREEN MEAL

LEANS	GREENS	CONDIMENTS

MOOD / ENERGY

SLEEP _____ HRS.   WATER ⚪⚪⚪⚪⚪ ⚪⚪⚪⚪

EXERCISE: NOTES

CARDIO	STRENGTH	FLEXIBILITY	OTHER

CRUSH IT!

M   T   W   T   F   S   S

1 Today's Date	2 Today's Weight	3 Weight Change from Yesterday

TODAY'S FUELINGS

1 _____

2 _____

3 _____

4 _____

5 _____

6 _____

Opt. Snack: _____

LEAN AND GREEN MEAL

LEANS	GREENS	CONDIMENTS

MOOD / ENERGY

SLEEP _____ HRS.   WATER ⬤⬤⬤⬤⬤ ⬤⬤⬤⬤⬤

EXERCISE:

NOTES

CARDIO	STRENGTH	FLEXIBILITY	OTHER

WEEK 3 DONE!

M T W T F S S

1 Today's Date	**2** Today's Weight	**3** Weight Change from Yesterday

TODAY'S FUELINGS

1 _____

2 _____

3 _____

4 _____

5 _____

6 _____

Opt. Snack: _____

LEAN AND GREEN MEAL

LEANS	GREENS	CONDIMENTS

MOOD / ENERGY

SLEEP _____ HRS.   WATER ⚪⚪⚪⚪⚪ ⚪⚪⚪⚪⚪

EXERCISE: NOTES

CARDIO	STRENGTH	FLEXIBILITY	OTHER

DON'T QUIT!

M   T   W   T   F   S   S

1 Today's Date	**2** Today's Weight	**3** Weight Change from Yesterday

TODAY'S FUELINGS

1 _____

2 _____

3 _____

4 _____

5 _____

6 _____

Opt. Snack: _____

LEAN AND GREEN MEAL

LEANS	GREENS	CONDIMENTS

MOOD / ENERGY

SLEEP _____ HRS.   WATER ⚪⚪⚪⚪⚪ ⚪⚪⚪⚪⚪

EXERCISE:

NOTES

CARDIO	STRENGTH	FLEXIBILITY	OTHER

YOU'RE INCREDIBLE!

M T W T F S S

1 Today's Date	2 Today's Weight	3 Weight Change from Yesterday

TODAY'S FUELINGS

1 _____

2 _____

3 _____

4 _____

5 _____

6 _____

Opt. Snack: _____

LEAN AND GREEN MEAL

LEANS	GREENS	CONDIMENTS

MOOD / ENERGY

SLEEP _____ HRS.   WATER ○○○○○ ○○○○○

EXERCISE: NOTES

CARDIO	STRENGTH	FLEXIBILITY	OTHER

KEEP IT UP!

M   T   W   T   F   S   S

1 Today's Date	**2** Today's Weight	**3** Weight Change from Yesterday

TODAY'S FUELINGS

1 _____

2 _____

3 _____

4 _____

5 _____

6 _____

Opt. Snack: _____

LEAN AND GREEN MEAL

LEANS	GREENS	CONDIMENTS

MOOD / ENERGY

SLEEP _____ HRS.   WATER ⚪⚪⚪⚪⚪ ⚪⚪⚪⚪⚪

EXERCISE: NOTES

CARDIO	STRENGTH	FLEXIBILITY	OTHER

BE SO PROUD!

M   T   W   T   F   S   S

1 Today's Date	**2** Today's Weight	**3** Weight Change from Yesterday

TODAY'S FUELINGS

1 _____

2 _____

3 _____

4 _____

5 _____

6 _____

Opt. Snack: _____

LEAN AND GREEN MEAL

LEANS	GREENS	CONDIMENTS

MOOD / ENERGY

SLEEP _____ HRS.   WATER ●●●●● ●●●●●

EXERCISE:

NOTES

CARDIO	STRENGTH	FLEXIBILITY	OTHER

ALMOST THERE!

M T W T F S S

1 Today's Date	**2** Today's Weight	**3** Weight Change from Yesterday

TODAY'S FUELINGS

1 _____

2 _____

3 _____

4 _____

5 _____

6 _____

Opt. Snack: _____

LEAN AND GREEN MEAL

LEANS	GREENS	CONDIMENTS

MOOD / ENERGY

SLEEP _____ HRS.   WATER ○○○○○ ○○○○○

EXERCISE:

CARDIO	STRENGTH	FLEXIBILITY	OTHER

NOTES

CELEBRATE YOU!

M   T   W   T   F   S   S

1 Today's Date	2 Today's Weight	3 Weight Change from Yesterday

TODAY'S FUELINGS

1 _____

2 _____

3 _____

4 _____

5 _____

6 _____

Opt. Snack: _____

LEAN AND GREEN MEAL

LEANS	GREENS	CONDIMENTS

MOOD / ENERGY

SLEEP _____ HRS.   WATER ○ ○ ○ ○ ○
                                  ○ ○ ○ ○

EXERCISE: NOTES

CARDIO	STRENGTH	FLEXIBILITY	OTHER

MONTH ONE DONE!

M   T   W   T   F   S   S

1 Today's Date	**2** Today's Weight	**3** Weight Change from Yesterday

TODAY'S FUELINGS

1 _____

2 _____

3 _____

4 _____

5 _____

6 _____

Opt. Snack: _____

LEAN AND GREEN MEAL

LEANS	GREENS	CONDIMENTS

MOOD / ENERGY

SLEEP _____ HRS.   WATER ● ● ● ● ●
● ● ● ● ●

EXERCISE: NOTES

CARDIO	STRENGTH	FLEXIBILITY	OTHER

MONTH 1 PROGRESS

STATS

BEFORE	
Weight	:
BMI	:
Body Fat	:
Muscle	:
Size.	:

AFTER	
Weight	:
BMI	:
Body Fat	:
Muscle	:
Size	:

MEASUREMENTS

BEFORE	
Chest	:
Waist	:
Hips	:
Arms	:
Thighs	:
Calves	:

AFTER	
Chest	:
Waist	:
Hips	:
Arms	:
Thighs	:
Calves	:

MOTIVATION

Pounds I lost this month

GOAL WEIGHT

RIGHT ON TRACK!

M T W T F S S

1 Today's Date	**2** Today's Weight	**3** Weight Change from Yesterday

TODAY'S FUELINGS

1 _____

2 _____

3 _____

4 _____

5 _____

6 _____

Opt. Snack: _____

LEAN AND GREEN MEAL

LEANS	GREENS	CONDIMENTS

MOOD / ENERGY

SLEEP _____ HRS.   WATER ⬤⬤⬤⬤⬤ ⬤⬤⬤⬤⬤

EXERCISE:

NOTES

CARDIO	STRENGTH	FLEXIBILITY	OTHER

EXCELLENT !

M T W T F S S

1 Today's Date	2 Today's Weight	3 Weight Change from Yesterday

TODAY'S FUELINGS

1 _____

2 _____

3 _____

4 _____

5 _____

6 _____

Opt. Snack: _____

LEAN AND GREEN MEAL

LEANS	GREENS	CONDIMENTS

MOOD / ENERGY

SLEEP _____ HRS.   WATER ⬤⬤⬤⬤⬤ ⬤⬤⬤⬤⬤

EXERCISE:

NOTES

CARDIO	STRENGTH	FLEXIBILITY	OTHER

MOVING RIGHT ALONG !

M T W T F S S

1 Today's Date	**2** Today's Weight	**3** Weight Change from Yesterday

TODAY'S FUELINGS

1 _____

2 _____

3 _____

4 _____

5 _____

6 _____

Opt. Snack: _____

LEAN AND GREEN MEAL

LEANS	GREENS	CONDIMENTS

MOOD / ENERGY

SLEEP _____ HRS.   WATER ● ● ● ● ●
　　　　　　　　　　　　　　　　　　　 ● ● ● ● ●

EXERCISE: NOTES

CARDIO	STRENGTH	FLEXIBILITY	OTHER

YOU'RE DOING GREAT !

M   T   W   T   F   S   S

1 Today's Date	**2** Today's Weight	**3** Weight Change from Yesterday

TODAY'S FUELINGS

1 _____

2 _____

3 _____

4 _____

5 _____

6 _____

Opt. Snack: _____

LEAN AND GREEN MEAL

LEANS	GREENS	CONDIMENTS

MOOD / ENERGY

SLEEP _____ HRS.   WATER ○○○○○ ○○○○○

EXERCISE: NOTES

CARDIO	STRENGTH	FLEXIBILITY	OTHER

CRUSHIN' GOALS !

M   T   W   T   F   S   S

1 Today's Date	**2** Today's Weight	**3** Weight Change from Yesterday

TODAY'S FUELINGS

1 _____

2 _____

3 _____

4 _____

5 _____

6 _____

Opt. Snack: _____

LEAN AND GREEN MEAL

LEANS	GREENS	CONDIMENTS

MOOD / ENERGY

SLEEP _____ HRS.   WATER ⚪⚪⚪⚪⚪
⚪⚪⚪⚪⚪

EXERCISE: NOTES

CARDIO	STRENGTH	FLEXIBILITY	OTHER

IMPRESSIVE !

M   T   W   T   F   S   S

1	Today's Date	2	Today's Weight	3	Weight Change from Yesterday

TODAY'S FUELINGS

1 _____

2 _____

3 _____

4 _____

5 _____

6 _____

Opt. Snack: _____

LEAN AND GREEN MEAL

LEANS	GREENS	CONDIMENTS

MOOD / ENERGY

SLEEP _____ HRS.   WATER ⚪⚪⚪⚪⚪
⚪⚪⚪⚪⚪

EXERCISE: NOTES

CARDIO	STRENGTH	FLEXIBILITY	OTHER

WEEK 5 DONE !

M   T   W   T   F   S   S

1 Today's Date	**2** Today's Weight	**3** Weight Change from Yesterday

TODAY'S FUELINGS

1 _____

2 _____

3 _____

4 _____

5 _____

6 _____

Opt. Snack: _____

LEAN AND GREEN MEAL

LEANS	GREENS	CONDIMENTS

MOOD / ENERGY

SLEEP _____ HRS.   WATER ○○○○ ○○○○

EXERCISE:

NOTES

CARDIO	STRENGTH	FLEXIBILITY	OTHER

MAKE IT HAPPEN !

M   T   W   T   F   S   S

1 Today's Date	**2** Today's Weight	**3** Weight Change from Yesterday

TODAY'S FUELINGS

1 _____

2 _____

3 _____

4 _____

5 _____

6 _____

Opt. Snack: _____

LEAN AND GREEN MEAL

LEANS	GREENS	CONDIMENTS

MOOD / ENERGY

SLEEP _____ HRS.   WATER ⚪⚪⚪⚪⚪ ⚪⚪⚪⚪⚪

EXERCISE:

NOTES

CARDIO	STRENGTH	FLEXIBILITY	OTHER

DOING FINE !

M T W T F S S

1 Today's Date	**2** Today's Weight	**3** Weight Change from Yesterday

TODAY'S FUELINGS

1 _____

2 _____

3 _____

4 _____

5 _____

6 _____

Opt. Snack: _____

LEAN AND GREEN MEAL

LEANS	GREENS	CONDIMENTS

MOOD / ENERGY

SLEEP _____ HRS.   WATER ⚪⚪⚪⚪⚪ ⚪⚪⚪⚪⚪

EXERCISE: NOTES

CARDIO	STRENGTH	FLEXIBILITY	OTHER

CLIMBIN' MOUNTAINS !

M   T   W   T   F   S   S

1 Today's Date	**2** Today's Weight	**3** Weight Change from Yesterday

TODAY'S FUELINGS

1 _____

2 _____

3 _____

4 _____

5 _____

6 _____

Opt. Snack: _____

LEAN AND GREEN MEAL

LEANS	GREENS	CONDIMENTS

MOOD / ENERGY

SLEEP _____ HRS.   WATER ⬤⬤⬤⬤⬤ ⬤⬤⬤⬤⬤

EXERCISE:

NOTES

CARDIO	STRENGTH	FLEXIBILITY	OTHER

SMASHING GOALS !

M   T   W   T   F   S   S

1 Today's Date	**2** Today's Weight	**3** Weight Change from Yesterday

TODAY'S FUELINGS

1 _____

2 _____

3 _____

4 _____

5 _____

6 _____

Opt. Snack: _____

LEAN AND GREEN MEAL

LEANS	GREENS	CONDIMENTS

MOOD / ENERGY

SLEEP _____ HRS.   WATER ⚪⚪⚪⚪⚪ ⚪⚪⚪⚪⚪

EXERCISE: NOTES

CARDIO	STRENGTH	FLEXIBILITY	OTHER

JUST KEEP MOVING !

M   T   W   T   F   S   S

1 Today's Date	**2** Today's Weight	**3** Weight Change from Yesterday

TODAY'S FUELINGS

1 _____

2 _____

3 _____

4 _____

5 _____

6 _____

Opt. Snack: _____

LEAN AND GREEN MEAL

LEANS	GREENS	CONDIMENTS

MOOD / ENERGY

SLEEP _____ HRS.   WATER ○○○○○ ○○○○○

EXERCISE:

NOTES

CARDIO	STRENGTH	FLEXIBILITY	OTHER

GREAT JOB !

M   T   W   T   F   S   S

1 Today's Date	**2** Today's Weight	**3** Weight Change from Yesterday

TODAY'S FUELINGS

1 _____

2 _____

3 _____

4 _____

5 _____

6 _____

Opt. Snack: _____

LEAN AND GREEN MEAL

LEANS	GREENS	CONDIMENTS

MOOD / ENERGY

SLEEP _____ HRS.   WATER ⚪⚪⚪⚪⚪ ⚪⚪⚪⚪⚪

EXERCISE:

NOTES

CARDIO	STRENGTH	FLEXIBILITY	OTHER

WEEK 6 DONE !

M   T   W   T   F   S   S

1 Today's Date	**2** Today's Weight	**3** Weight Change from Yesterday

TODAY'S FUELINGS

1 _____

2 _____

3 _____

4 _____

5 _____

6 _____

Opt. Snack: _____

LEAN AND GREEN MEAL

LEANS	GREENS	CONDIMENTS

MOOD / ENERGY

SLEEP _____ HRS.   WATER ○○○○○ ○○○○○

EXERCISE:

CARDIO	STRENGTH	FLEXIBILITY	OTHER

NOTES

YOU'VE GOT THIS !

M   T   W   T   F   S   S

1 Today's Date	**2** Today's Weight	**3** Weight Change from Yesterday

TODAY'S FUELINGS

1 _____

2 _____

3 _____

4 _____

5 _____

6 _____

Opt. Snack: _____

LEAN AND GREEN MEAL

LEANS	GREENS	CONDIMENTS

MOOD / ENERGY

SLEEP _____ HRS.   WATER ⚪⚪⚪⚪⚪ ⚪⚪⚪⚪⚪

EXERCISE: NOTES

CARDIO	STRENGTH	FLEXIBILITY	OTHER

FANTASTIC WORK !

M   T   W   T   F   S   S

1 Today's Date	**2** Today's Weight	**3** Weight Change from Yesterday

TODAY'S FUELINGS

1 _____

2 _____

3 _____

4 _____

5 _____

6 _____

Opt. Snack: _____

LEAN AND GREEN MEAL

LEANS	GREENS	CONDIMENTS

MOOD / ENERGY

SLEEP _____ HRS.   WATER ⚪⚪⚪⚪⚪ ⚪⚪⚪⚪⚪

EXERCISE:

NOTES

CARDIO	STRENGTH	FLEXIBILITY	OTHER

BREAK THAT LEVEL !

M   T   W   T   F   S   S

1 Today's Date	**2** Today's Weight	**3** Weight Change from Yesterday

TODAY'S FUELINGS

1 _____

2 _____

3 _____

4 _____

5 _____

6 _____

Opt. Snack: _____

LEAN AND GREEN MEAL

LEANS	GREENS	CONDIMENTS

MOOD / ENERGY

SLEEP _____ HRS.   WATER ⚪⚪⚪⚪⚪ ⚪⚪⚪⚪

EXERCISE: NOTES

CARDIO	STRENGTH	FLEXIBILITY	OTHER

POSTITIVE THINKING !

M   T   W   T   F   S   S

1 Today's Date	**2** Today's Weight	**3** Weight Change from Yesterday

TODAY'S FUELINGS

1 _____

2 _____

3 _____

4 _____

5 _____

6 _____

Opt. Snack: _____

LEAN AND GREEN MEAL

LEANS	GREENS	CONDIMENTS

MOOD / ENERGY

SLEEP _____ HRS.   WATER ⚪⚪⚪⚪⚪ ⚪⚪⚪⚪

EXERCISE: NOTES

CARDIO	STRENGTH	FLEXIBILITY	OTHER

WORK IT !

M T W T F S S

1 Today's Date	2 Today's Weight	3 Weight Change from Yesterday

TODAY'S FUELINGS

1 _____

2 _____

3 _____

4 _____

5 _____

6 _____

Opt. Snack: _____

LEAN AND GREEN MEAL

LEANS	GREENS	CONDIMENTS

MOOD / ENERGY

SLEEP _____ HRS.   WATER ⚪⚪⚪⚪⚪ ⚪⚪⚪⚪⚪

EXERCISE:

NOTES

CARDIO	STRENGTH	FLEXIBILITY	OTHER

YEAH, BABY !

M T W T F S S

1 Today's Date	**2** Today's Weight	**3** Weight Change from Yesterday

TODAY'S FUELINGS

1 _____

2 _____

3 _____

4 _____

5 _____

6 _____

Opt. Snack: _____

LEAN AND GREEN MEAL

LEANS	GREENS	CONDIMENTS

MOOD / ENERGY

SLEEP _____ HRS.   WATER ○○○○○ ○○○○○

EXERCISE:

CARDIO	STRENGTH	FLEXIBILITY	OTHER

NOTES

WEEK 7 DONE !

M T W T F S S

1 Today's Date	**2** Today's Weight	**3** Weight Change from Yesterday

TODAY'S FUELINGS

1 _____

2 _____

3 _____

4 _____

5 _____

6 _____

Opt. Snack: _____

LEAN AND GREEN MEAL

LEANS	GREENS	CONDIMENTS

MOOD / ENERGY

SLEEP _____ HRS.   WATER ⚪⚪⚪⚪⚪ ⚪⚪⚪⚪⚪

EXERCISE:

NOTES

CARDIO	STRENGTH	FLEXIBILITY	OTHER

START STRONG !

M T W T F S S

1 Today's Date	**2** Today's Weight	**3** Weight Change from Yesterday

TODAY'S FUELINGS

1 _____

2 _____

3 _____

4 _____

5 _____

6 _____

Opt. Snack: _____

LEAN AND GREEN MEAL

LEANS	GREENS	CONDIMENTS

MOOD / ENERGY

SLEEP _____ HRS.   WATER ○○○○○ ○○○○

EXERCISE:

NOTES

CARDIO	STRENGTH	FLEXIBILITY	OTHER

YOU CAN DO IT !

M T W T F S S

1 Today's Date	2 Today's Weight	3 Weight Change from Yesterday

TODAY'S FUELINGS

1 _____

2 _____

3 _____

4 _____

5 _____

6 _____

Opt. Snack: _____

LEAN AND GREEN MEAL

LEANS	GREENS	CONDIMENTS

MOOD / ENERGY

SLEEP _____ HRS.   WATER ⚪⚪⚪⚪⚪ ⚪⚪⚪⚪⚪

EXERCISE: NOTES

CARDIO	STRENGTH	FLEXIBILITY	OTHER

YOU ARE INCREDIBLE !

M   T   W   T   F   S   S

1 Today's Date	**2** Today's Weight	**3** Weight Change from Yesterday

TODAY'S FUELINGS

1 _____

2 _____

3 _____

4 _____

5 _____

6 _____

Opt. Snack: _____

LEAN AND GREEN MEAL

LEANS	GREENS	CONDIMENTS

MOOD / ENERGY

SLEEP _____ HRS.   WATER ○○○○○ ○○○○○

EXERCISE:

NOTES

CARDIO	STRENGTH	FLEXIBILITY	OTHER

DESTROYING TARGETS !

M   T   W   T   F   S   S

1 Today's Date	2 Today's Weight	3 Weight Change from Yesterday

TODAY'S FUELINGS

1 _____

2 _____

3 _____

4 _____

5 _____

6 _____

Opt. Snack: _____

LEAN AND GREEN MEAL

LEANS	GREENS	CONDIMENTS

MOOD / ENERGY

SLEEP _____ HRS.   WATER ⚪⚪⚪⚪⚪ ⚪⚪⚪⚪⚪

EXERCISE:

NOTES

CARDIO	STRENGTH	FLEXIBILITY	OTHER

STAY ON TRACK !

M   T   W   T   F   S   S

1 Today's Date	2 Today's Weight	3 Weight Change from Yesterday

TODAY'S FUELINGS

1 _____

2 _____

3 _____

4 _____

5 _____

6 _____

Opt. Snack: _____

LEAN AND GREEN MEAL

LEANS	GREENS	CONDIMENTS

MOOD / ENERGY

SLEEP _____ HRS.   WATER ○○○○○ ○○○○○

EXERCISE: NOTES

CARDIO	STRENGTH	FLEXIBILITY	OTHER

KICKIN' BUTT !

M   T   W   T   F   S   S

1 Today's Date	2 Today's Weight	3 Weight Change from Yesterday

TODAY'S FUELINGS

1 _____

2 _____

3 _____

4 _____

5 _____

6 _____

Opt. Snack: _____

LEAN AND GREEN MEAL

LEANS	GREENS	CONDIMENTS

MOOD / ENERGY

SLEEP _____ HRS.   WATER ○○○○○ ○○○○○

EXERCISE:

NOTES

CARDIO	STRENGTH	FLEXIBILITY	OTHER

WEEK 8 DONE !

M T W T F S S

1 Today's Date	**2** Today's Weight	**3** Weight Change from Yesterday

TODAY'S FUELINGS

1 _____

2 _____

3 _____

4 _____

5 _____

6 _____

Opt. Snack: _____

LEAN AND GREEN MEAL

LEANS	GREENS	CONDIMENTS

MOOD / ENERGY

SLEEP _____ HRS.   WATER ⚪⚪⚪⚪⚪ ⚪⚪⚪⚪

EXERCISE:

CARDIO	STRENGTH	FLEXIBILITY	OTHER

NOTES

MONTH 2 PROGRESS

STATS

BEFORE	
Weight	:
BMI	:
Body Fat	:
Muscle	:
Size.	:

AFTER	
Weight	:
BMI	:
Body Fat	:
Muscle	:
Size	:

MEASUREMENTS

BEFORE	
Chest	:
Waist	:
Hips	:
Arms	:
Thighs	:
Calves	:

AFTER	
Chest	:
Waist	:
Hips	:
Arms	:
Thighs	:
Calves	:

MOTIVATION	Pounds I lost this month	GOAL WEIGHT

ON YOUR MARK !

M   T   W   T   F   S   S

1 Today's Date   **2** Today's Weight   **3** Weight Change from Yesterday

TODAY'S FUELINGS

1 _____

2 _____

3 _____

4 _____

5 _____

6 _____

Opt. Snack: _____

LEAN AND GREEN MEAL

LEANS	GREENS	CONDIMENTS

MOOD / ENERGY

SLEEP _____ HRS.   WATER ⦿⦿⦿⦿⦿ ⦿⦿⦿⦿⦿

EXERCISE:

NOTES

CARDIO	STRENGTH	FLEXIBILITY	OTHER

YOU ARE SET !

M   T   W   T   F   S   S

1 Today's Date	**2** Today's Weight	**3** Weight Change from Yesterday

TODAY'S FUELINGS

1 _____

2 _____

3 _____

4 _____

5 _____

6 _____

Opt. Snack: _____

LEAN AND GREEN MEAL

LEANS	GREENS	CONDIMENTS

MOOD / ENERGY

SLEEP _____ HRS.   WATER ⚪⚪⚪⚪⚪ ⚪⚪⚪⚪

EXERCISE: NOTES

CARDIO	STRENGTH	FLEXIBILITY	OTHER

PUNCH IT UP !

M T W T F S S

1 Today's Date	**2** Today's Weight	**3** Weight Change from Yesterday

TODAY'S FUELINGS

1 _____

2 _____

3 _____

4 _____

5 _____

6 _____

Opt. Snack: _____

LEAN AND GREEN MEAL

LEANS	GREENS	CONDIMENTS

MOOD / ENERGY

SLEEP _____ HRS.   WATER ⚪⚪⚪⚪⚪ ⚪⚪⚪⚪

EXERCISE:

NOTES

CARDIO	STRENGTH	FLEXIBILITY	OTHER

KEEP IT GOING !

M   T   W   T   F   S   S

1 Today's Date	**2** Today's Weight	**3** Weight Change from Yesterday

TODAY'S FUELINGS

1 _____

2 _____

3 _____

4 _____

5 _____

6 _____

Opt. Snack: _____

LEAN AND GREEN MEAL

LEANS	GREENS	CONDIMENTS

MOOD / ENERGY

SLEEP _____ HRS.   WATER ⚪⚪⚪⚪⚪ ⚪⚪⚪⚪⚪

EXERCISE:

NOTES

CARDIO	STRENGTH	FLEXIBILITY	OTHER

YOU ARE ASTONISHING !

M   T   W   T   F   S   S

1 Today's Date	2 Today's Weight	3 Weight Change from Yesterday

TODAY'S FUELINGS

1 _____

2 _____

3 _____

4 _____

5 _____

6 _____

Opt. Snack: _____

LEAN AND GREEN MEAL

LEANS	GREENS	CONDIMENTS

MOOD / ENERGY

SLEEP _____ HRS.   WATER ⬤⬤⬤⬤⬤ ⬤⬤⬤⬤⬤

EXERCISE:

NOTES

CARDIO	STRENGTH	FLEXIBILITY	OTHER

FEEL THE LOVE !

M T W T F S S

1 Today's Date	**2** Today's Weight	**3** Weight Change from Yesterday

TODAY'S FUELINGS

1 _____

2 _____

3 _____

4 _____

5 _____

6 _____

Opt. Snack: _____

LEAN AND GREEN MEAL

LEANS	GREENS	CONDIMENTS

MOOD / ENERGY

SLEEP _____ HRS.   WATER ⚪⚪⚪⚪⚪ ⚪⚪⚪⚪⚪

EXERCISE: NOTES

CARDIO	STRENGTH	FLEXIBILITY	OTHER

WEEK 9 DONE !

M   T   W   T   F   S   S

1 Today's Date	**2** Today's Weight	**3** Weight Change from Yesterday

TODAY'S FUELINGS

1 _____

2 _____

3 _____

4 _____

5 _____

6 _____

Opt. Snack: _____

LEAN AND GREEN MEAL

LEANS	GREENS	CONDIMENTS

MOOD / ENERGY

SLEEP _____ HRS.   WATER ○○○○○ ○○○○○

EXERCISE: NOTES

CARDIO	STRENGTH	FLEXIBILITY	OTHER

LET'S GO !

M   T   W   T   F   S   S

1 Today's Date	**2** Today's Weight	**3** Weight Change from Yesterday

TODAY'S FUELINGS

1 _____

2 _____

3 _____

4 _____

5 _____

6 _____

Opt. Snack: _____

LEAN AND GREEN MEAL

LEANS	GREENS	CONDIMENTS

MOOD / ENERGY

SLEEP _____ HRS.   WATER ⚪⚪⚪⚪⚪ ⚪⚪⚪⚪⚪

EXERCISE:

NOTES

CARDIO	STRENGTH	FLEXIBILITY	OTHER

KICK IT UP !

M T W T F S S

1 Today's Date	**2** Today's Weight	**3** Weight Change from Yesterday

TODAY'S FUELINGS

1 _____

2 _____

3 _____

4 _____

5 _____

6 _____

Opt. Snack: _____

LEAN AND GREEN MEAL

LEANS	GREENS	CONDIMENTS

MOOD / ENERGY

SLEEP _____ HRS.   WATER ⚪⚪⚪⚪⚪ ⚪⚪⚪⚪⚪

EXERCISE:

NOTES

CARDIO	STRENGTH	FLEXIBILITY	OTHER

MOVING FORWARD !

M   T   W   T   F   S   S

1 Today's Date	**2** Today's Weight	**3** Weight Change from Yesterday

TODAY'S FUELINGS

1 _____

2 _____

3 _____

4 _____

5 _____

6 _____

Opt. Snack: _____

LEAN AND GREEN MEAL

LEANS	GREENS	CONDIMENTS

MOOD / ENERGY

SLEEP _____ HRS.   WATER ○○○○○ ○○○○

EXERCISE:

NOTES

CARDIO	STRENGTH	FLEXIBILITY	OTHER

SMASHING PROGRESS !

M   T   W   T   F   S   S

1 Today's Date	**2** Today's Weight	**3** Weight Change from Yesterday

TODAY'S FUELINGS

1 _____

2 _____

3 _____

4 _____

5 _____

6 _____

Opt. Snack: _____

LEAN AND GREEN MEAL

LEANS	GREENS	CONDIMENTS

MOOD / ENERGY

SLEEP _____ HRS.   WATER ○ ○ ○ ○
○ ○ ○ ○

EXERCISE:

NOTES

CARDIO	STRENGTH	FLEXIBILITY	OTHER

YOU ARE A STAR !

M T W T F S S

1 Today's Date	**2** Today's Weight	**3** Weight Change from Yesterday

TODAY'S FUELINGS

1 _____

2 _____

3 _____

4 _____

5 _____

6 _____

Opt. Snack: _____

LEAN AND GREEN MEAL

LEANS	GREENS	CONDIMENTS

MOOD / ENERGY

SLEEP _____ HRS.   WATER ⬤⬤⬤⬤⬤ ⬤⬤⬤⬤⬤

EXERCISE:

NOTES

CARDIO	STRENGTH	FLEXIBILITY	OTHER

MAKING CHANGES !

M T W T F S S

1 Today's Date	2 Today's Weight	3 Weight Change from Yesterday

TODAY'S FUELINGS

1 _____

2 _____

3 _____

4 _____

5 _____

6 _____

Opt. Snack: _____

LEAN AND GREEN MEAL

LEANS	GREENS	CONDIMENTS

MOOD / ENERGY

SLEEP _____ HRS.   WATER ○○○○○ ○○○○

EXERCISE:

NOTES

CARDIO	STRENGTH	FLEXIBILITY	OTHER

WEEK 10 DONE !

M   T   W   T   F   S   S

1 Today's Date	2 Today's Weight	3 Weight Change from Yesterday

TODAY'S FUELINGS

1 _____

2 _____

3 _____

4 _____

5 _____

6 _____

Opt. Snack: _____

LEAN AND GREEN MEAL

LEANS	GREENS	CONDIMENTS

MOOD / ENERGY

SLEEP _____ HRS.   WATER ⬤⬤⬤⬤⬤ ⬤⬤⬤⬤

EXERCISE:

NOTES

CARDIO	STRENGTH	FLEXIBILITY	OTHER

YOU ARE BEAUTIFUL !

M   T   W   T   F   S   S

1	Today's Date	2	Today's Weight	3	Weight Change from Yesterday

TODAY'S FUELINGS

1 _____

2 _____

3 _____

4 _____

5 _____

6 _____

Opt. Snack: _____

LEAN AND GREEN MEAL

LEANS	GREENS	CONDIMENTS

MOOD / ENERGY

SLEEP _____ HRS.   WATER ○○○○○ ○○○○○

EXERCISE: NOTES

CARDIO	STRENGTH	FLEXIBILITY	OTHER

BE PROUD OF YOU !

M T W T F S S

1 Today's Date	**2** Today's Weight	**3** Weight Change from Yesterday

TODAY'S FUELINGS

1 _____

2 _____

3 _____

4 _____

5 _____

6 _____

Opt. Snack: _____

LEAN AND GREEN MEAL

LEANS	GREENS	CONDIMENTS

MOOD / ENERGY

SLEEP _____ HRS.   WATER ⬤⬤⬤⬤⬤ ⬤⬤⬤⬤⬤

EXERCISE:

NOTES

CARDIO	STRENGTH	FLEXIBILITY	OTHER

HARD WORKS PAYS OFF !

M   T   W   T   F   S   S

1 Today's Date	**2** Today's Weight	**3** Weight Change from Yesterday

TODAY'S FUELINGS

1 _____

2 _____

3 _____

4 _____

5 _____

6 _____

Opt. Snack: _____

LEAN AND GREEN MEAL

LEANS	GREENS	CONDIMENTS

MOOD / ENERGY

SLEEP _____ HRS.   WATER ○○○○○ ○○○○○

EXERCISE: NOTES

CARDIO	STRENGTH	FLEXIBILITY	OTHER

KEEP ON PLAN !

M T W T F S S

1 Today's Date	**2** Today's Weight	**3** Weight Change from Yesterday

TODAY'S FUELINGS

1 _____

2 _____

3 _____

4 _____

5 _____

6 _____

Opt. Snack: _____

LEAN AND GREEN MEAL

LEANS	GREENS	CONDIMENTS

MOOD / ENERGY

SLEEP _____ HRS.   WATER ○○○○○ ○○○○○

EXERCISE:

CARDIO	STRENGTH	FLEXIBILITY	OTHER

NOTES

SMASHING GOALS !

M T W T F S S

1 Today's Date	2 Today's Weight	3 Weight Change from Yesterday

TODAY'S FUELINGS

1 _____

2 _____

3 _____

4 _____

5 _____

6 _____

Opt. Snack: _____

LEAN AND GREEN MEAL

LEANS	GREENS	CONDIMENTS

MOOD / ENERGY

SLEEP _____ HRS.   WATER ○○○○○ ○○○○○

EXERCISE: NOTES

CARDIO	STRENGTH	FLEXIBILITY	OTHER

BUILDING BETTER !

M   T   W   T   F   S   S

1 Today's Date	**2** Today's Weight	**3** Weight Change from Yesterday

TODAY'S FUELINGS

1 _____

2 _____

3 _____

4 _____

5 _____

6 _____

Opt. Snack: _____

LEAN AND GREEN MEAL

LEANS	GREENS	CONDIMENTS

MOOD / ENERGY

SLEEP _____ HRS.   WATER ○ ○ ○ ○ ○
○ ○ ○ ○ ○

EXERCISE:

NOTES

CARDIO	STRENGTH	FLEXIBILITY	OTHER

WEEK 11 DONE !

M   T   W   T   F   S   S

1 Today's Date	**2** Today's Weight	**3** Weight Change from Yesterday

TODAY'S FUELINGS

1 _____

2 _____

3 _____

4 _____

5 _____

6 _____

Opt. Snack: _____

LEAN AND GREEN MEAL

LEANS	GREENS	CONDIMENTS

MOOD / ENERGY

SLEEP _____ HRS.   WATER ○ ○ ○ ○ ○ ○ ○ ○ ○

EXERCISE: NOTES

CARDIO	STRENGTH	FLEXIBILITY	OTHER

CHANGE IS GOOD !

M   T   W   T   F   S   S

1 Today's Date	2 Today's Weight	3 Weight Change from Yesterday

TODAY'S FUELINGS

1 _____

2 _____

3 _____

4 _____

5 _____

6 _____

Opt. Snack: _____

LEAN AND GREEN MEAL

LEANS	GREENS	CONDIMENTS

MOOD / ENERGY

SLEEP _____ HRS.   WATER ○○○○○ ○○○○○

EXERCISE:

NOTES

CARDIO	STRENGTH	FLEXIBILITY	OTHER

YOU'RE DOING GREAT !

M   T   W   T   F   S   S

1 Today's Date	2 Today's Weight	3 Weight Change from Yesterday

TODAY'S FUELINGS

1 _____

2 _____

3 _____

4 _____

5 _____

6 _____

Opt. Snack: _____

LEAN AND GREEN MEAL

LEANS	GREENS	CONDIMENTS

MOOD / ENERGY

SLEEP _____ HRS.   WATER ⚪⚪⚪⚪⚪ ⚪⚪⚪⚪⚪

EXERCISE:

NOTES

CARDIO	STRENGTH	FLEXIBILITY	OTHER

FLEX THOSE MUSCLES !

M   T   W   T   F   S   S

1 Today's Date	**2** Today's Weight	**3** Weight Change from Yesterday

TODAY'S FUELINGS

1 _____

2 _____

3 _____

4 _____

5 _____

6 _____

Opt. Snack: _____

LEAN AND GREEN MEAL

LEANS	GREENS	CONDIMENTS

MOOD / ENERGY

SLEEP _____ HRS.   WATER ⚪⚪⚪⚪⚪ ⚪⚪⚪⚪⚪

EXERCISE: NOTES

CARDIO	STRENGTH	FLEXIBILITY	OTHER

SHRINKING SIZES !

M T W T F S S

1 Today's Date	**2** Today's Weight	**3** Weight Change from Yesterday

TODAY'S FUELINGS

1 _____

2 _____

3 _____

4 _____

5 _____

6 _____

Opt. Snack: _____

LEAN AND GREEN MEAL

LEANS	GREENS	CONDIMENTS

MOOD / ENERGY

SLEEP _____ HRS.   WATER ○○○○○ ○○○○

EXERCISE:

NOTES

CARDIO	STRENGTH	FLEXIBILITY	OTHER

STUNNING PROGRESS !

M   T   W   T   F   S   S

1 Today's Date	**2** Today's Weight	**3** Weight Change from Yesterday

TODAY'S FUELINGS

1 _____

2 _____

3 _____

4 _____

5 _____

6 _____

Opt. Snack: _____

LEAN AND GREEN MEAL

LEANS	GREENS	CONDIMENTS

MOOD / ENERGY

SLEEP _____ HRS.   WATER ○○○○○ ○○○○○

EXERCISE:

NOTES

CARDIO	STRENGTH	FLEXIBILITY	OTHER

SHOWING OFF !

M   T   W   T   F   S   S

1 Today's Date	**2** Today's Weight	**3** Weight Change from Yesterday

TODAY'S FUELINGS

1 _____

2 _____

3 _____

4 _____

5 _____

6 _____

Opt. Snack: _____

LEAN AND GREEN MEAL

LEANS	GREENS	CONDIMENTS

MOOD / ENERGY

SLEEP _____ HRS.   WATER ○○○○○ ○○○○

EXERCISE:

NOTES

CARDIO	STRENGTH	FLEXIBILITY	OTHER

WEEK 12 DONE ! WHOA!

M T W T F S S

1 Today's Date	**2** Today's Weight	**3** Weight Change from Yesterday

TODAY'S FUELINGS

1 _____

2 _____

3 _____

4 _____

5 _____

6 _____

Opt. Snack: _____

LEAN AND GREEN MEAL

LEANS	GREENS	CONDIMENTS

MOOD / ENERGY

SLEEP _____ HRS.   WATER ○○○○○ ○○○○○

EXERCISE: NOTES

CARDIO	STRENGTH	FLEXIBILITY	OTHER

MONTH 3 PROGRESS

STATS

BEFORE	
Weight	:
BMI	:
Body Fat	:
Muscle	:
Size.	:

AFTER	
Weight	:
BMI	:
Body Fat	:
Muscle	:
Size	:

MEASUREMENTS

BEFORE	
Chest	:
Waist	:
Hips	:
Arms	:
Thighs	:
Calves	:

AFTER	
Chest	:
Waist	:
Hips	:
Arms	:
Thighs	:
Calves	:

MOTIVATION

Pounds I lost this month

GOAL WEIGHT

YOU DID IT!

You should be so proud of you!
Let's celebrate!

Pounds lost in 3 Months:

Sizes lost in 3 Months:

Cardio Fitness I Gained:

Strength Training I Gained:

Made in the USA
Las Vegas, NV
13 May 2023

72023239R00052